employment is crucial and was of benefit to all of our attendees. Ty received excellent feedback on his presentation. Finally, he was cool and calm in the midst of a technical crisis during his time slot! I highly recommend Ty as a speaker for your HR or recruiting conference or event."

— **Andrea Ballard, WA State SHRM 2021 Conference Director**

"This eye-opening book will make you rethink your hiring policies and practices. As Ty Reed reveals, one in three American adults today has a criminal record. That is a huge chunk of the workforce you don't want to ignore when looking for possible candidates. Many of those people are highly skilled and they are all looking for a second chance. Ty dispels the myths about the negative consequences of hiring those with criminal pasts and he enumerates the many benefits that result when you give people a second chance. They will repay you with loyalty and hard work, a win-win for everyone. Read this book and open your mind to the possibilities."

— **Tyler R. Tichelaar, PhD and Award-Winning Author of**
*Narrow Lives* **and** *The Best Place*

'story' is and get the whole picture. With more than seventy-seven-million candidates with criminal records, this would help us reach our hiring targets, have a bench, and then help people get back on their feet when all they need is a chance to prove themselves. This process Ty has created would also help organizations reach both their hiring and DE&I targets. It was an enlightening presentation, and I would recommend Ty Reed as a speaker for SHRM and other professional organizations and as a consultant for your business."

— Jennifer Pigeon, Speaker Chair for
AZ State SHRM Conference 2022

"I so appreciate hearing Ty's story and reframing work processes like recruitment and hiring to incorporate more equitable approaches that support people."

— Amber Santoyo, Chief People Officer,
Washington State Department of Health

"Ty Reed captivated our audience with his deep and broad experience, his passion for inclusion, and his great love for humanity. We all left the session with more hope, both as employers and as members of society."

— Holly Eckert, South Puget Sound SHRM Programs Director

"I've had the pleasure of attending a couple of presentations by Ty and have found them to be both informative and inspirational. We are committed to continuing and increasing our impact to the communities we work in, and Ty's experience and knowledge have given us additional pathways to meet this goal. Ty is seen as a valuable community partner, and we look forward to partnering with him in the future."

— Arhonda Reyes, WA State SHRM Director - DEI

"Ty Reed was an exceptional speaker at our annual Washington State SHRM HR Conference. His  message of providing second chance

# What People Are Saying About Ty Reed and *Second Chance Hiring*

"Some people have a harder time than others in creating their own destinies. Ty Reed understands that, which is why he has written this book to encourage employers to provide those with criminal records a second chance. Everyone wants to feel valued and have a fair chance at contributing to society and making their world better. More importantly for employers, Ty reveals that second chance hiring has innumerable benefits from providing a larger pool of qualified workers to hiring long-term and loyal employees. This book will revolutionize your HR department and your business."

— **Patrick Snow, Publishing Coach and International Best-Selling Author of *Creating Your Own Destiny* and *The Affluent Entrepreneur***

"If you hire or make hiring decisions, you *must* hear Ty Reed."

— **Marianne Ozmun-Wells, Equity and Inclusion Office Administrator**

"As the speaker committee chair for the Arizona SHRM Conference, Ty Reed's personal story really struck me. How many other professionals out there in our workplaces have dealt with addiction and successfully beat it after being incarcerated? Ty spoke to us about biases that exist in the hiring process and how by asking more questions and being more curious, we can better understand whether a candidate is a good fit for the position. In this time when we have a constant shortage of good candidates, Ty shared some statistics on one of the biggest labor pools we ignore, the individuals with criminal records. He gave us some tools to enable us to ask better questions and to stop assuming what we think the

# SECOND CHANCE HIRING

## Human Resources Strategies to Lower Your Risk Through Inclusive Recruiting

## TY REED

# Dedication

To Heather, Phillip, Angela, Taj, Myra, Bill,
and Marcella for never giving up on me.

# Acknowledgments

Thank you to the following people for helping or inspiring me to complete this book:

Patrick Snow for your endless encouragement, expertise, and advice.

Author Jeffrey Korzenik for his book *Untapped Talent*, which strongly advocates for second chance hiring.

Johnny C. Taylor, Jr., CEO of the Society of Human Resource Management (SHRM) and the organization itself for being vocal proponents of inclusive hiring practices.

What's Next WA, Pioneer Human Services, The Second Chance Business Coalition, the WA Statewide Reentry Council, and other community-based organizations that continue to champion the cause of providing opportunities for those with criminal records.

Marcella Reed for being generous with your legal expertise (and for always giving me the family discount).

And to the thousands of HR practitioners working every day to do the right thing.

# Contents

# Introduction

I didn't really know I had a drug problem until one of my dealers told me he was worried about me!

That's the truth. I had always thought of myself as someone who "liked to party." The problem was I liked to party until I was homeless.

Early in my sales career, a mentor told me, "Success is a wonderful deodorant." I didn't know what he meant then, but he was talking about how we often allow professional and financial success to cover up whatever "stink" may be happening in our personal lives. Back in 2007, that was exactly the situation I found myself in.

As a sales and business development professional in financial services for a division of a Fortune 50 company, I had just received national recognition as a salesperson in the top 10 percent, which brought me great visibility and respect, and a pretty nice paycheck. My second wife and I had bought a new, large, and expensive house in Seattle's northern suburbs. We were blessed with plenty of money in the bank and no debt. My wonderful, funny, and talented stepdaughter, who lived with us part-time, was enrolled in a private school and, by all appearances, seemed happy. If you had simply taken a snapshot of my life then, it would have been a beautiful—and incomplete—picture.

You see, I also had been carrying a secret for five years — one I would carry for many more. I was living a double life. By day, I was an accomplished employee, a so-so stepfather, and a horrible husband. By night, I was an alcoholic and crack cocaine addict, which contributed heavily to my deficiencies as a stepparent and spouse.

The stress of this double life was exhausting, and I often thought about suicide, but I never stopped to consider making a real effort at change. I rationalized that things couldn't be that bad if I was doing so well at work. I used my hefty income to justify the suffering I put my wife through and the absenteeism my stepdaughter endured. That income also fed my always-needy ego. I had long felt like an outsider, and being able to achieve and earn so much professionally acted as a salve for the wounded self-esteem and low self-worth I had carried for most of my life.

Then the 2008 recession shook my world. The company I worked for shut down my division, and the same happened at many similar companies. Suddenly, my income was gone. Unfortunately, so was much of our savings, squandered by me on drugs and alcohol. What wasn't gone was my addiction.

The loss of my job made it impossible for me to hide my substance issues, and the toll on the family grew. My wife left me not long after I lost my job, not because I lost my steady source of income, but because she finally did what she should have done many years earlier. She recognized I was toxic and not ready to do anything about it. I was a good salesperson, and the best sales job I ever did was convincing her I could be a good partner. Her decision to leave was the right one.

We soon lost the beautiful new house and moved into separate apartments. Although my ex-wife was open to me continuing a relationship with my stepdaughter, my inability to stay clean again forced her hand. I lost that relationship and didn't see or speak to my stepdaughter for ten years. The last time I saw my stepdaughter, I told her I loved her, but prior to entering recovery, I couldn't be a positive adult in her life. I kissed and hugged her, went out to my car, and cried so uncontrollably

I almost got into an accident on the way back to my apartment. And then I went and got high.

Recently, I ran across an interview with David Lee Roth, the former lead singer of Van Halen who was talking about the time after he left the band (or was fired, depending on whom you believe). He said something that rang so true for me (I'm paraphrasing): "When you're making a bunch of money, and you have a drug habit, it's not really an issue. But when the money goes away, and the habit doesn't, that's when you've got a drug problem."

Over the next few years, I worked and had some moderate level of success, but I never reached the professional heights I had before. I even managed to complete an MBA program in 2009, but the drug and alcohol use were taking their toll. I had a couple of failed stints in rehab and continued to spiral.

In 2012, I decided to get off crack…by switching to meth.

I never said my decision-making was good, but meth was an effective way to quit crack.

That decision ranks right up there with deciding to lose weight by cutting off your arm. It'll work, but it ain't smart.

Life got pretty dismal after that. While I had somehow managed to work, keep a non-drug-using group of friends, and hold my life together somewhat while smoking crack for ten years, meth changed everything. Soon, my social circle consisted of dealers, thugs, hustlers, hookers, and pimps. My ability to work was significantly undermined. And then things turned incredibly dark.

In June of 2014, I found myself unemployed, unable to hold a job, more heavily addicted to drugs and alcohol than ever, and homeless. I had no idea where my next meal would come from or where I would sleep next. I had also burned all my family relationships and friendships to the ground.

And I was relieved.

By that point, I felt like my daytime professional persona was all an act. Plus, it was getting in the way of my using drugs. Once I lost everything, I could finally just be one person—and that person needed booze and meth.

Over the next couple of years, I would get the full experience of being a homeless drug addict. I know regular folks look at people experiencing homelessness and assume they are lazy. The unhoused may be lots of things, but lazy is not one of them. Being homeless and unemployed was the hardest job I ever had. It was a constant struggle with no weekends, holidays, or paid time off—just the unrelenting pressure of existing on society's fringes.

I would have another failed stint in rehab. Later, after being high and awake for days, I would have a mental episode and be committed to a psychiatric facility for a time. Because I had no legal source of income, I would commit petty crimes daily to earn money, and I ended up arrested, convicted, and jailed multiple times.

I was also lucky enough to survive a couple of suicide attempts.

Like I said, things got dark.

When I had finally had enough of the suffering I caused myself and my family, I entered recovery in 2016 and began rebuilding life. It has been a long, slow process that has included several relapses, and the support of many people. Today, I am grateful to have what, by any measure, is a fulfilling life with work I enjoy, a deep connection with friends and family, and the ability to help others taking the same journey I took.

In June 2020, I started a nonprofit, Recovery Career Services, which focuses on helping others put their lives back together by providing employment support. Initially, I was simply providing no-cost career coaching for individuals going through all kinds of job-related stresses due to substance use (past or present), homelessness, and incarceration.

Recovery Career Services has since expanded programming to provide support for those in early recovery or newly released from incarceration who need help finding and keeping work.

In support of this nonprofit, it has become an honor and a privilege to speak to human resources professionals and businesses about the importance of second chance hiring. While attitudes about hiring from this population have softened over the past few years, I am still amazed by the stigma and resistance those with criminal convictions face when looking for employment.

The difficulties I faced after getting sober inspired me to help others. Through pain, I have found purpose. The journey here has not been without its ups and downs. One of the most challenging things I did was rebuild my career.

When I entered recovery, I was a very odd mix of stuff. On the positive side, I had a decade of great work history, an MBA from one of the finest universities in the United States, and I interviewed well.

On the negative side, I hadn't worked for two years, had horrible credit, (which would, no doubt, have been revealed on a background check), and multiple criminal convictions. These days, due to the pandemic, a two-year job gap doesn't mean much, but back in 2016 when I began looking for work again, that gap was a major red flag.

But it was the criminal history that caused me the most trouble in restarting my career, even though all I had were misdemeanors.

The purpose of this book is to bring attention to the difficulties people who have been involved in the criminal justice system experience and to highlight why employers who don't currently hire from this pool should rethink that position.

In this book's title and many times throughout, the phrase "second chance hiring" will be used. This refers to evaluating and hiring workers with criminal histories that would appear on a background check.

This phrase also includes the set of policies and procedures an organization must put in place to support this practice.

I sincerely hope that after reading this book, you will better understand why second chance hiring presents a tremendous opportunity for employers, job seekers, and communities, and you will be inspired to take action and hire one (or many more) of these candidates when you encounter them.

# 1

## Ground Rules

Before jumping into the meat of this book, I want to familiarize you with some assumptions and terms and make a disclaimer.

I assume you have at least some basic knowledge of human resources practices and how a good HR practitioner can influence an organization. I also assume you will approach this text in good faith, with an open heart and willingness to listen (and maybe even learn). Second chance hiring can be a charged topic, especially if the reader has had personal and/or professional experiences with this population.

Much of the legal basis for considering second chance hiring comes from the Equal Employment Opportunity Commission's (EEOC) 2012 guidance regarding how employers should treat applicants who have criminal convictions.[1] This is an incredibly important guidance because it lays the framework that will help companies remain compliant and avoid possible costly litigation. During my consulting work, I have spoken with many organizations and HR professionals who know of this guidance but have not taken active steps to ensure they are fully compliant when hiring (or not hiring) someone with a criminal record.

---

1    US Employment Opportunity Commission. "Enforcement Guidance on the Consideration of Arrest and Conviction Records in Employment Decisions under Title VII of the Civil Rights Act." https://www.eeoc.gov/laws/guidance/enforcement-guidance-consideration-arrest-and-conviction-records-employ-ment-decisions. Accessed February 1, 2023.

Two terms are used, often interchangeably, but I want to make a distinction here. I do not believe that "fair chance hiring" and "second chance hiring" are the same thing.

If you do a search on LinkedIn Jobs, you will notice a filter for companies that identify themselves as "fair chance employers." While this is a nice marketing piece for LinkedIn and employers who self-identify in this category, this designation can be meaningless in many cases.

All that "fair chance" really means is the company does not ask about criminal history on the job application. Often, that is not because the organization has made a moral decision to have this policy; at the time of this writing, many states, cities, and municipalities have instituted "fair chance hiring" laws (alternatively called "ban the box" laws), removing the question about criminal history from applications and defining when a company can ask job seekers about this part of their pasts.

However, fair chance legislation doesn't say anything about whether a company can run a background check or whether the organization has to hire anyone with a criminal record. Based on reports from job seekers with these backgrounds, many organizations are still using criminal histories to deny employment, even in circumstances where the background is unrelated to the position applied for.

In other words, these companies use background checks to "screen out" people.

Alternatively, true "second chance employers" make it their policy to hire from this pool of applicants. MOD Pizza, the fastest-growing restaurant in America for many years, is a beautiful example of this. They hire people with almost any criminal background, have established internal and external support for their workers, and have been rewarded with steady growth, profits, and employee loyalty.

## Second Chance Success Story: MOD Pizza[2]

MOD Pizza, recognized by Nation's Restaurant News as the fastest-growing US restaurant chain in terms of sales for two consecutive years, prioritizes its employees' growth over mere financial milestones. The company proudly brands itself as a "second chance employer." However, this philosophy isn't exclusive to former inmates, even though they make up roughly 21 percent of MOD Pizza's workforce.

Kory Harp, the program manager for impact hires at MOD Pizza, explains their philosophy: "MOD gives a second chance to everybody. Whether it's a mother returning to work after a long hiatus or a teenager taking on their first job to support their college dreams, MOD offers opportunities indiscriminately."

But MOD is not just about pizza. Their business approach reflects their motto of "Spreading MODness," which focuses on taking care of their employees, so they, in turn, care for the customers, ensuring the business thrives. This strategy seems successful as reflected in their sales growth of 44.7 percent in 2018 and their expansion from thirty-one outlets in 2014 to 476 across twenty-nine states, the UK, and Canada today.

The uniqueness of MOD's approach began with Harp. After being released from prison around 2010, Harp joined MOD Pizza. The hiring manager saw potential in him, despite his incarceration. Harp recalls, "The boss told me to hire more people like me who had the same kind of background." MOD's emphasis on hiring those with a criminal record became more pronounced three years after Harp's hiring. Today, in the state of Washington, where MOD is based, up to 66 percent of some

---

2    Jails to Jobs. "MOD Pizza Finds Strength as Second Chance Employer." https://jailstojobs.org/mod-pizza-finds-strength-as-second-chance-employer/. Accessed February 1, 2023.

districts' residents employed by the company have criminal records. Nationally, this figure stands at 18 to 21 percent for the company.

Harp's original plan to work at MOD for a few months turned into a tenure spanning more than a decade. In his time, he has launched ninety-one MOD stores and trained countless employees nationwide. Currently, he's working on establishing a mentorship program to assist employees in managing life challenges, whether they stem from reintegration after prison, addiction recovery, or any other personal struggle.

While details of the mentorship program remain under wraps, Harp hints at a significant partner supporting the initiative. As MOD continues its expansion, its core mission remains unchanged: maintain the unique culture, ensure employee happiness, and give back to the communities they serve.

||||||||||||||||||||||||||||||||||

## Exercise

What is one thing you learned from this section of the book? How will this affect the way you think about hiring people with criminal convictions?

_____

_____

_____

_____

How does this book's perspective on this issue compare with your own beliefs or experiences prior to reading this section?

_____

_____

_____

_____

## Second Chance Success Story:
## Pallet Shelter[3]

Amy King, CEO of Pallet Shelter in Everett, Washington, articulates her firm belief not only in the tangible product they make—shelters for the homeless—but more so in the workforce-development model her company has embraced. King asserts that their primary mission extends beyond mere product manufacturing, focusing on creating living-wage jobs, and nurturing skill sets that will enable people to flourish.

Despite their successful product line, King imparts a conviction that may seem radical to many business owners: broadening the employee recruiting landscape to consider individuals who've experienced hardship, including homelessness, addiction, or encounters with the criminal justice system. She passionately explains, "Four walls and a roof do not solve displacement. It's about job opportunities, economic stability, and wealth generation. That's the magic that's going to create sustainable solutions."

In an unorthodox but empowering approach, King prefers to hire those who have found it challenging to secure and keep regular jobs. Many of her staff have had a brush with the justice system, a fact she openly acknowledges. Through her experiences working with such individuals, she attests to their brilliance, intelligence, creativity, and productivity. They are, in her words, "some of the most...productive citizens I've ever met."

King acknowledges that prejudices and regulations often inhibit these individuals from breaking free from the vicious cycle of poverty and homelessness. Yet she firmly believes in the transformational power of employment, saying, "Offering someone a job is a very simple way of saying, 'We believe in you.'"

---

3    "Prefab Pallet Shelters and Dignified Work Address Homelessness Holistically." https://redshift.autodesk.com/articles/pallet-shelters. Accessed July 19, 2023.

While the approach has been met with skepticism from traditional businesses, King stands her ground. She believes the key to dismantling human bias lies in introducing different populations to one another. Her company strives to foster this intermingling, taking employees from varying backgrounds into corporate settings to share their stories and challenge misconceptions.

Recalling an outdated standard where hiring individuals with felony backgrounds was an absolute no-go, King provocatively asks, "Why not?" She emphasizes that these individuals are not inherently bad people. Many respond positively to rehabilitation efforts and are willing to change if given the opportunity.

King fervently encourages the potential in these individuals, fostering it through meaningful employment, housing, and community. She envisions a world where everyone is given the chance to change and grow, shifting from merely surviving to genuinely thriving. The Pallet shelters are not just about offering temporary refuge; they symbolize a commitment to sparking a societal shift and providing sustainable solutions to homelessness and displacement.

||||||||||||||||||||||||||||||||||||

These second chance employers recognize immense talent exists in the large pool of people with criminal records. They are putting policies in place to "screen in" people, providing great opportunities for individuals and the organization.

People often ask me what the correct terminology is when referring to people with criminal convictions. We all know the importance of "person first" language, so we definitely want to avoid stigmatizing words such as:

- Felon

- Convict

- Criminal

- Crook

- Jailbird

Acceptable terms I use interchangeably are person or individual:

- Impacted by the criminal justice system.

- With previous criminal justice involvement.

- With criminal convictions.

- With a criminal history.

Or the phrase "justice-involved person."

Any of the above are acceptable when speaking about individuals within this population.

When we speak about the effects of the criminal justice system, we must also discuss race.

It is not my intent for this book to discuss the causes of this skewed justice or level any systemic accusations. I simply present data as facts. And those facts should also be considered when you are crafting hiring policies that seek to exclude those with past criminal justice involvement. While your intent may be to prevent people with criminal convictions from being employed within your organization, communities of color have been disproportionately affected by the criminal justice system. People of color are incarcerated at rates five times higher than white people.[4] Comparative sentencing studies show that a person of color receives a sentence 10 percent longer than a white offender with a similar criminal history for the same crime.[5]

---

4    NAACP. "Criminal Justice Fact Sheet." https://naacp.org/resources/criminal-justice-fact-sheet. Accessed February 1, 2023.

5    Rehavi, M. Marit and Sonja B. Starr. "Racial Disparity in Federal Criminal Sentences." Michigan Law, University of Michigan. https://repository.law.umich.edu/articles/1414/. Accessed February 1, 2023.

In response to this national epidemic, the EEOC has determined that deciding an individual applicant's status based on their prior involvement with the criminal justice system without further inquiry and/or appropriate justification may be a form of disparate treatment—discrimination on the basis of race or national origin. The EEOC has also pointed out that having a blanket policy that excludes from hiring consideration all applicants with criminal backgrounds, even though neutral on its face, is likely to affect people of color more frequently than whites, causing it to have a disparate impact and making it unlawful.

Therefore, the fairest, safest, and most effective solution is striving to craft the most inclusive hiring policies possible while balancing your business' needs.

You will find success stories sprinkled throughout the book that highlight employers who have made a shift to second chance hiring, along with stories of community-based organizations that serve this population of job seekers. I hope you find inspiration and similarities that spark creative ways to begin these practices at your organization.

These second chance stories highlight that it is not only possible to hire from this population of talented job seekers, but possible for your organization to grow, thrive, and make a huge impact in the community, all while remaining profitable.

And finally, I've included exercises and reflection questions at the end of each section for you to consider. I believe to get the full benefit of reading this book, you should pause and take a few minutes to complete them before moving to the next section. These activities will deepen your understanding as you finish the book and consider how your company can institute some of the hiring practices you will learn.

# 2

## A Few Words About Second Chances

In many parts of the world, second chances have become harder to come by. With the rise of social media, it has become a regular practice for total strangers to try to ruin people or institutions for minor transgressions or simple mistakes.

Even worse, those on social media regularly go back ten or twenty years to look at what a person said or did long ago and use it as evidence an individual should be shunned. Besides not being a very compassionate practice, this process looks at the worst moment, day, words, or acts of someone's life without context. Judging another person in this way leaves no room for them to be what they likely are: complicated. People are not all one thing, and they are not the sum total of one thing they said or one act they committed.

Every good person has done some bad things; conversely, every bad person has some done some good. At some point in our lives, we will all need to be given grace for some act we committed. We should also give grace. Unfortunately, we often judge, fail to see nuance in situations, and impose our standards on others.

While it may make us feel superior or righteous, all it really does is create distance between us and the people we deem to be less worthy because of some past errors in judgment or expression. We hate it when people do it to us, so why do we do this to those around us?

Having hiring practices where the totality of a person is considered recognizes that often people need grace instead of judgment. This is especially true when people actively try to live differently than they had before.

Grace gives us an opportunity to catch people doing the right things now, instead of punishing them for the wrong things they did in the past.

## Second Chance Success Story: US Rubber Recycling

Carlos Arceo, now thriving as the second-shift manager at US Rubber Recycling in Colton, California, epitomizes the untapped potential of individuals with criminal backgrounds. In merely two years post-release, Carlos has remarkably advanced in his career, garnering respect and a promising future.

However, many like Carlos face limited opportunities. With approximately seventy-seven-million Americans having a criminal record, post-sentence societal marginalization, unemployment, and poverty are common, often leading back to crime. The Second Chance Business Coalition actively endorses hiring these individuals, underscoring mutual benefits.

Jeff Baldassari, CEO of US Rubber and Recyling, states, "Merely opening doors isn't enough; creating conducive environments where these individuals can genuinely thrive is essential. Since 2019, leading a team where half have criminal records, I've learned a lot."

Here are Baldassari's key lessons:

1. **Overcome Bias:** It's vital not to let prejudices dictate hiring decisions. Carlos's hiring, although unconventional given his age and lack of experience, proved invaluable.

2. **Foster Inclusivity:** Ex-convicts, post-release, often grapple with financial challenges, fractured relationships, and societal disdain. "Judging them by their past is a mistake. Recognizing their present potential is pivotal," asserts Baldassari.

3. **Prioritize Positivity:** The power of positive reinforcement can't be overstated. Many ex-convicts are used to negative feedback. Celebrating their efforts and progressively trusting them with more responsibilities fosters growth and trust.

4. **Champion Teamwork:** Former inmates often adopt a self-centered survival mentality. To counter this, promoting a collaborative ethos is vital. "Incorporating their feedback and ensuring they grasp their role's value can enhance team dynamics," Baldassari notes.

5. **Engage Specialists:** "Our collaboration with Nancy Lambert, a psychiatric rehabilitation counselor, has been game-changing," Baldassari remarks. "As their full-time HR manager, Nancy aids our employees, especially those incarcerated young, in navigating personal and professional challenges, given their often limited life skills exposure."

6. **Accept Potential Hurdles:** Not all second chance employees will thrive. Despite initial achievements, some find consistency challenging. Baldassari candidly shares, "Their turnover can be disheartening, but witnessing successes like Carlos's is immeasurably rewarding, showcasing the resilience of the human spirit."

|||||||||||||||||||||||||||||||||||||||

## Exercise

Think back on your life. In three to five sentences, write down an example of when you were given a second chance.

_____

_____

_____

_____

How did that second chance make you feel? What are some words or phrases you would use to describe your feelings?

_____

_____

_____

# 3

# COVID, Big Numbers, and Luck

Depending on which article you read, somewhere between two and three million people took early retirement during the COVID pandemic. Millions more of non-retirement age who experienced layoffs during the early days of the pandemic have either not returned to the workforce or have switched jobs. What are a few of the reasons job openings have returned, but workers have not?

- **COVID-19:** Despite the presence of widely available vaccines, many front-line workers are seeking alternatives to their former jobs.

- **Less available daycare:** During the pandemic, sixteen-thousand daycare centers permanently closed.[1] Workers are in short supply. Fewer workers and social distancing requirements mean fewer spots available for kids.

- **Finances:** Even if you can find a spot for your child in daycare, unless you see a clear financial advantage to going back to work and paying for childcare instead of staying home, there is no incentive to justify the risks. If your child gets sick or there is a COVID outbreak at the daycare, it closes, and arrange-

---

1  Leonhardt, Megan. "16,000 Childcare Providers Shut Down in the Pandemic. It's a Really Big Deal." *Fortune Magazine*. February 2022. https://fortune.com/2022/02/09/child-care-providers-shut-down-pandemic/. Accessed February 1, 2023.

ments must be made, likely meaning you or your spouse will need time off from work. This also goes for school-age children. Additionally, with the shortage of daycare centers, the price of daycare has gone up dramatically.

- **New business openings:** In 2021, 5.4 million new businesses opened,[2] a 20-plus percent increase over pre-pandemic numbers, with trends showing even more businesses would open in 2022.

- **The side hustle/gig economy:** Many workers have been able to make a good living with side hustles like driving for rideshare services like Lyft or Uber or working as independent contractors from home on sites such as Fiverr. For near-minimum wage frontline workers, these are wage replacement positions with much more flexibility than a traditional job. Many labor industry experts also suspect more people than ever are working under the table.

What this situation means for employers is open positions are up, retention rates are down, and much of the power in the labor market now lies with job seekers and employees.

Many labor market analysts (and workers) say this is good for employees overall. In an effort to attract and retain workers, many employers have been forced to increase pay and benefits. Between March of 2021 and August of 2022, the average hourly wage rose by 7.6 percent. (Unfortunately, this hasn't kept pace with inflation, meaning real wages

---

2    US Census Bureau Business Formation Statistics. https://www.census.gov/econ/currentdata/dbsearch?programCode=BFS&startYear=2021&endYear=2021&categories[]=TOTAL&dataType=BA_BA&geoLevel=US&adjusted=1&notAdjusted=1&errorData=0. Accessed February 1, 2023.

have actually fallen.)[3] The competition between employers—even those from dissimilar industries—to attract workers has grown fierce.

But what about employers who feel they cannot pay these higher wages or cover the costs of enhanced benefits for entry-level positions? (Here, I am being generous and assuming employers truly *can't* pay, instead of going with the suspicions of many that employers simply *won't* pay.) Yes, they could focus on their culture and make employees feel like "family." These are worthy endeavors for any employer and can help bring about long-term changes to a company. But what about the employer that needs workers yesterday? Is there an easy solution? (Hint: This book's title should give you a clue.)

Many employers fail to realize the huge opportunity they are missing by maintaining policies that exclude those with criminal backgrounds. The applicant pool is large and companies are self-limiting by ignoring a great deal of talent.

The US has an incarceration problem. It is, by far, the highest incarceration rate in the world.[4] Additionally, its system of laws is simply byzantine. On top of all that, in many lower-income neighborhoods—black, brown, and white—there is often a heightened (and aggressive) police presence.

These factors make it easy for a huge chunk of the population to come in contact with law enforcement regularly. And the more contact you have with police, the greater the likelihood you'll end up in the system. According to the National Conference of State Legislatures (NCSL), approximately seventy-seven-million adults in the United States have

---

3    Forbes. "U.S. Wage Growth Fails to Keep Up With Rising Prices for 17 Consecutive Months." https://www.forbes.com/sites/qai/2022/10/01/us-wage-growth-fails-to-keep-up-with-rising-prices-for-17-consecutive-months/?sh=45476990b007. Accessed February 1, 2023.

4    Prison Policy Initiative. https://www.prisonpolicy.org/profiles/US.html. Accessed February 1, 2023.

a criminal record.[5] That works out to one in three adults. As a matter of fact, the number of people with conviction records is roughly the same as the number of people with bachelor's degrees.[6]

And while most employers may think of someone with a criminal record as a hardened, violent felon, the reality is that at any given time, about 80 percent of the cases on court dockets around the country are for nonviolent misdemeanors.[7]

I'm by no means saying that every person who comes into contact with law enforcement gets arrested or that everyone who gets arrested is innocent. I am saying the difference between someone with a criminal record and someone without one often comes down to luck and location.

Don't believe me? Let's take a quiz.

Think back on your life and ask yourself if you've ever:

- Had too much to drink and driven anyway?

- Shoplifted or stole something but didn't get caught? Or were caught and let off due to your family connections or because those involved felt "you had learned your lesson"?

- Gotten into a physical altercation with another person?

---

5    Criminal Records and Reentry, NCSL. https://www.ncsl.org/research/civil-and-criminal-justice/criminal-records-and-reentry. Accessed February 1, 2023.

6    Friedmann, Matthew. "Just Facts: As Many Americans Have Criminal Records as College Diplomas." https://www.brennancenter.org/our-work/analysis-opinion/just-facts-many-americans-have-criminal-records-college-diplomas. Accessed February 1, 2023.

7    New York University. "Prosecuting Nonviolent Misdemeanors Increases Rearrest Rates, New Study Shows." https://www.nyu.edu/about/news-publications/news/2021/march/prosecuting-nonviolent-misdemeanors-increases-rearrest-rates--ne.html. Accessed February 1, 2023.

- Ever consumed or been in possession of illegal drugs (including weed before it was legal in your state) or drank alcohol before age twenty-one?

If you said yes to any of these, but don't have a criminal record for DUI, theft, assault, or drug or alcohol possession, then you were lucky, and probably in the right place at the right time instead of the wrong place at the wrong time.

The perceptions of why and how people end up with criminal records directly influences companies' bias toward applicants with those records.

## Second Chance Success Story: Dave's Killer Bread[8]

In 2005, after serving fifteen years in prison, Dave Dahl returned to the family bakery business founded by his father in 1955. Once a high school dropout who disliked the bakery, Dave's newfound dedication not only reinvigorated his passion but also birthed the renowned Dave's Killer Bread.

Upon Dave's discovering a unique, organic, nutty bread recipe, the brand surged in popularity. Starting with thirty employees, it expanded to 190 by 2010 and 280 by 2012. Notably, Dave made a conscious choice to hire ex-convicts, understanding their challenges first-hand. "I was a four-time loser before I realized I was in the wrong game," Dave remarked.

By 2015, the business's success led to a $275 million acquisition by Flower Foods. Despite the change in ownership, the brand's core ethos remained unchanged, maintaining its advocacy for second chances and continuing its practice of hiring ex-convicts.

Dave's Killer Bread's popularity isn't solely due to its social impact. Recognized across the US and Canada, the bread, known for its whole grain ingredients and protein-rich content, stands out on store shelves. It holds the title of the best-selling organic, Non-GMO verified bread.

Beyond producing top-tier bread, Dave's Killer Bread's true essence lies in its commitment to "Second Chance Employment." While Dave found redemption through the family business, many ex-convicts aren't as fortunate, often facing societal obstacles upon release. This company doesn't just offer employment; it provides an avenue for personal trans-formation and community impact.

---

8    Second Chance employment for ex-cons at Dave's Killer Bread, https:// racinelaw.com/second-chance-employment-for-ex-cons-at-daves-killer-bread/. Accessed July 19, 2023.

Dave firmly believes in offering opportunities beyond past mistakes. A statement from their website encapsulates their mission: "At Dave's Killer Bread, we believe in Second Chance Employment: hiring the best person for the job, regardless of criminal history. [...] a Second Chance—gives people an opportunity not only to make a living but to make a life."

Unlike many businesses wary of criminal records, Dave's Killer Bread proudly shares that one-third of its workforce comprises individuals with criminal backgrounds. The company doesn't just see past records; it recognizes potential, passion, and commitment. These employees, with their transformative journeys, are often among the most valued, even ascending to managerial roles. Dave's story isn't just about personal redemption; it's about extending that chance to hundreds of others.

| | | | | | | | | | | | | | | | | | | | | | | | | | | | | | | | | | | | | | |

## Exercise

Have you ever done something that could have limited the opportunities you have today? What was it?

_____

_____

_____

_____


Why didn't it negatively affect you? What were the circumstances that allowed you to avoid serious repercussions?

_____

_____

_____

_____

# 4

# The Problem with the Box

While the pandemic provided a tremendous opportunity for companies to reach into the pool of overlooked and untapped talent, I recognize that someday, an employer will be reading this volume in a "post-pandemic" world. The labor force will have either returned to something close to its previous state or companies will have adapted to the new reality of workforce development.

Regardless of the state of the labor market, second chance hiring should always be part of your company's recruitment strategy. If a company is truly committed to building the strongest, most capable, and most experienced workforce possible, it must be prepared to evaluate every qualified candidate, regardless of source.

One of the primary functions of human resources is to help companies mitigate risks associated with human capital. To do this, organizations and HR departments have instituted a number of practices to remove some of the risks associated with hiring. Two of those practices directly influence inclusion in hiring.

The first is a section on job applications asking if an applicant has been convicted of a crime and then requesting information about the convictions. The second is pre-employment checks—including address history, credit scores, education verification, and criminal background screening—which are a standard part of many organizations' hiring process.

While these practices have certainly helped companies lessen some of the risks associated with hiring, like many things, they have also had profound secondary—and perhaps intended—effects.

The practice of asking if an applicant has had any criminal convictions during the application process has been a significant impediment to applicants getting to the first interview. A 2016 study performed by researchers from Rutgers and the University of Michigan found that "the criminal record effect" profoundly reduces the likelihood an applicant with a criminal record will be called for an interview.[1]

In this study, researchers filled out hundreds of employment applications in states that still asked about criminal convictions at the time of application. The researchers used a variety of personas with a number of variables, including race, gender, and industries. These characteristics included one group of applicants with no criminal record and a second group with low-level, nonviolent felony convictions two years before the application date.

The result? Controlling for all possible variables, applicants without criminal records were 60 percent more likely to get an interview request. These were not new findings. They confirmed the outcomes of other studies and demonstrated that employer perceptions excluded many people.

Fortunately, several states have enacted "Ban the Box" laws over the past few years. At the time of this writing, thirty-seven states and 150 cities, counties, and municipalities have passed laws that outline when

---

1    Agan, Amanda and Sonja B. Starr. "The Effect of Criminal Records on Access to Employment." University of Michigan Law School, 2017. https://repository.law.umich.edu/cgi/viewcontent.cgi?article=2892&context=articles. Accessed February 1, 2023.

an employer can ask about an applicant's criminal history.[2] While the specifics differ in each jurisdiction, the general premise is that by removing "the box" from the application process, more people—including those with criminal convictions—will be given an opportunity to interview and prove they are worthy of consideration for employment.

Clearly, the intent of banning the box is to help ensure more equal access to employment opportunities. And while intuitively one would think this increased access would automatically result in more people with criminal backgrounds finding employment, the outcome is decidedly mixed. According to a table published by the National Conference of State Legislatures, in some places, banning the box has made a significant difference, in some places, none, and in others, it has been detrimental to the hiring rates of people with criminal convictions.[3]

Why would this be?

Two factors could be at play: hearts and minds, and employer policy. What can never be controlled are: 1) the preconceived notions the interviewer or hiring manager has about people with criminal convictions; and 2) the guidelines companies have in place governing whether candidates with criminal backgrounds can be hired at all.

Each of us is simply a collection of our past experiences, and those experiences with people, places, and things define how we view situations and individuals. Although a hiring manager may be a good and generous person, if they have had a negative experience with someone with a criminal record, they likely have a negative view of all people with criminal records, and consciously or not, this bias may keep them from hiring from that population. In this way, even though ban the

---

2    National Employment Law Project, 2021. "Ban the Box: US Cities, Counties, and States Adopt Fair Hiring Policies." http://www.nelp.org/publication/ban-the-box-fair-chance-hiring-state-and-local-guide/. Accessed February 1, 2023.

3    NCSL. "Ban the Box." https://www.ncsl.org/research/civil-and-criminal-justice/ban-the-box. Accessed February 1, 2023.

box policies may get more people with criminal convictions interviews, if the company runs criminal background checks as a normal part of the hiring process, it is highly likely this manager's bias will be a factor in hiring.

To be fair, the bias could also be positive. If the hiring manager has a positive experience with a person with previous criminal justice involvement (perhaps the manager has seen a remarkable change in a relative and witnessed the full comeback the person has made), they may be predisposed to help those who have been negatively affected by the criminal justice system.

This is where company policy becomes the trump card. Even if the candidate with a criminal conviction is the best candidate, if company policy precludes hiring candidates for a certain period—it is common for companies to have a five- or seven-year moratorium on hiring individuals with criminal records—the manager's positive experience makes no difference. The result is still denied opportunity for an individual who may deserve it, and worse, the job seeker has gone through the entire process only to be rebuffed, costing them time and costing the company both time and money.

According to a study by the American Civil Liberties Union (ACLU), 75 percent of people will be unemployed one year after incarceration.[4] While many factors contribute to this, such as work experience prior to incarceration, education levels, and mental health, HR professional and hiring manager attitudes and employers' policies are likely the most important factors because they are the final barriers preventing individuals with criminal histories from finding work.

---

4    ACLU. "How Hiring Formerly Incarcerated Job Seekers Benefits Your Company." https://www.aclu.org/sites/default/files/field_document/060917-trone-reportweb_0.pdf. Accessed February 1, 2023.

## Second Chance Success Story: Nehemiah Manufacturing[5]

After serving thirty-three years in prison for aggravated robbery and murder, fifty-six-year-old Franklin Comer found his first job at Nehemiah Manufacturing in Cincinnati. During his time behind bars, Comer introspectively identified the flaws that led him to crime and worked toward bettering himself. "I knew I made a mistake. I tried to redeem myself into becoming a better person," he shared.

Upon release, Cincinnati Works, an Ohio-based job readiness organization, guided Comer toward societal reintegration, helping him obtain his driver's license and secure the position at Nehemiah. Now, as a warehouse associate, Comer is part of Nehemiah's significant portion of second chance hires, accounting for nearly 80 percent of its 180-strong workforce. This initiative is part of Nehemiah's decade-long commitment to inclusive capitalism. Comer appreciates the workplace atmosphere, noting, "They don't care about the past, [there's a] degree of compassion and understanding that they have here."

The drive toward hiring individuals with criminal records is not merely out of compassion. The manufacturing sector currently has half-a-million vacancies, a figure expected to rise to four million in the next decade. Addressing this need, The Manufacturing Institute and the Charles Koch Institute have partnered to promote second chance hiring opportunities, inspired by Nehemiah's successful model.

With one in three American adults having a criminal record, such initiatives are crucial. Carolyn Lee, The Manufacturing Institute's executive director, warns that failing to tap into this workforce could result in 2.1 million manufacturing jobs remaining unfilled over the next decade, potentially impacting the US economy with a trillion-dollar reduction in GDP by 2030. Lee emphasizes the high retention rates

---

5   Rogers, Kate and Stephanie Dhue. "Manufacturers Push to Give Workers with Criminal Records a Second Chance." https://www.cnbc.com/2021/05/07/manufacturers-push-to-give-workers-with-criminal-records-a-second-chance.html. Accessed February 1, 2023.

among second chance hires and their potential contribution to the industry.

Nehemiah Manufacturing's ethos extends beyond employment. Eric Wellinghoff, its chief marketing officer, highlights their holistic approach to supporting their staff, including providing on-site social services, housing, and transportation programs, like the "Wheels Program" which provided Comer with a car. In an industry known for high turnover, Nehemiah's staff averages a tenure of 5.5 years. "We have built a family here," Wellinghoff said.

The Manufacturing Institute is promoting modern manufacturing jobs as high-tech, clean, and lucrative, countering the outdated perception of the sector. They emphasize the attractive average annual salary of $84,000 and the above $15 hourly starting rate.

The emphasis on second chance hiring isn't limited to Nehemiah. The Beacon of Hope Business Alliance, initiated by Nehemiah Manufacturing in 2016, collaborates with companies like Kroger, Starbucks, and Home Depot, all of which maintain inclusive hiring practices for those with criminal records. Incentives like the federal Work Opportunity Tax Credit further motivate such hiring practices.

Comer's hope is that more firms will emulate Nehemiah's model. "When a man has truly become successful, it's because somebody believed in him and gave him a chance," he concludes.

| | | | | | | | | | | | | | | | | | | | | | | | | | | | | | | | | | | |

## Exercise

What personal beliefs might you be carrying that could inject bias (positive or negative) into the hiring process for people with criminal convictions?

_____

_____

_____

_____

Where do those beliefs come from?

_____

_____

_____

_____

What about your employer or your company? What beliefs or attitudes do ownership and/or management demonstrate that could limit opportunities for those affected by the criminal justice system?

_____

_____

_____

_____

# 5

# Finally, Something We Can All Agree Upon

In recent years, more attention has been paid to the difficulties people with criminal records have in finding work. During his time in office, President Obama was a proponent of the Second Chance Act, which provided grants and federal funding to nonprofits and agencies that assist those with past criminal justice involvement. And luckily, this is a bipartisan issue. In 2019, President Trump unveiled a program to encourage employers to hire formerly incarcerated individuals and reduce their unemployment rates to single digits by 2024. Pre-pandemic, the unemployment rate for individuals previously involved with the criminal justice system sat at 27 percent, while the overall unemployment rate hovered at around 4 percent.[1]

Why are employers still hesitant to hire the formerly incarcerated? It is likely due to the stigma and perception that criminals are more likely to be unreliable and be guilty of misconduct on the job. However, the real experience of companies who have hired from this population do not support this perception.

Let me say here that some second chance hires will not work out, just as is the case when hiring candidates without criminal backgrounds. Hiring any employee is a risk, and a 2018 study by the Society of

---

1    Couloute, Lucius and Daniel Kopf. "Out of Prison & Out of Work: Unemployment Among Formerly Incarcerated People." https://www.prison-policy.org/reports/outofwork.html. Accessed February 1, 2023.

Human Resource Management (SHRM, considered to be a liberal-leaning organization due to its stance on DEI—Diversity, Equity, and Inclusion strategies) and the Charles Koch Institute (the same Charles Koch who has donated tens of millions of dollars to conservative candidates and causes) surveyed 1,052 full-time employees, consisting of 540 managers (including C-Suite executives) and 512 non-managers, plus an additional 1,228 HR professionals. The study found compelling evidence that hiring from the pool of applicants with criminal backgrounds should be a part of the overall hiring strategy for companies.[2]

Of the organizations who hired workers with criminal records:

- More than 80 percent of managers and two-thirds of HR professionals feel the value workers with criminal records bring to the organization is as high or higher than that of workers without records.

- Three-quarters of managers and HR professionals believe the cost of hiring workers with criminal records is the same or lower than that of hiring workers without criminal records.

- A majority of workers in all roles say they are willing to work with individuals with criminal records, and an additional 30 to 40 percent report they are neutral on the subject.

- Among managers and HR professionals, a demonstrated consistent work history was the leading factor in their willingness to hire a worker with a criminal record.

- Top reasons for hiring workers with criminal records include a desire to hire the best candidate for the job regardless of criminal history, making the community a better place, and giving individuals a second chance.

2    SHRM. "Workers with Criminal Records." https://www.shrm.org/hr-today/trends-and-forecasting/research-and-surveys/pages/second-chances.aspx. Accessed February 1, 2023.

The first section of the last bullet is important: a desire to hire the best candidate for the job regardless of criminal history. If more employers would simply do this, many of the reservations surrounding second chance hiring would dissolve. While it would be great if all employers bought into making the community a better place and giving individuals a second chance, some employers may not see those reasons as business-driven. An employer would be hard-pressed to find a reason to deny an individual an opportunity if they were the best candidate.

Obviously, other issues need to be addressed to make it easier for these job seekers to find and keep employment, such as building an applicant's skills, providing networking opportunities, and more. But despite these other needed supports and resources, a commitment to choosing the best candidate, regardless of criminal background, would be a major step toward removing hurdles.

# Second Chance Success Story: Koch Industries

Many people might be surprised that one of the leading second chance employers in the US is part of a group of companies run by the conservative Koch family. According to John Buckley, who is the Outreach Programs Lead for all businesses in the Koch Industries conglomerate, in 2020 alone, the company hired more than eleven thousand individuals with past criminal convictions, which were a mix of both misdemeanors and felonies. While he would say that their second chance program has been a success, it hasn't been without challenges.

"One of the biggest initial challenges we faced was apprehension among the folks who lead business units. Their reaction was, 'I don't want folks you know who have been incarcerated on my team,'" he says. "The secondary one was how to properly assess the background information so that we're really considering the risk to the business in a fair way. And a third one was just the breadth of Koch Industries and getting the word out, as easy as you would think it is."

Despite these challenges, Koch has stayed the course and shown leadership in helping secure employment for those with criminal justice backgrounds. Besides direct hiring, Koch Industries has partnered with the Society for Human Resource Management (SHRM) to fund surveys, collect data about employers' feelings about hiring from this talent pool, and show the benefits when they do. Overwhelmingly, the data shows that worker quality and performance are as good or better when compared to workers without criminal convictions.

According to Buckley, Koch also does other things, like limiting their lookback period on felonies, evaluating past crimes using certain criteria such as the nature of the crime and whether it was a one-time or repeat offense, and allowing applicants to present information during the interview process that can be used to mitigate their pasts, such as whether or not they have entered recovery, gained education, or rehabilitated themselves in other ways since their last offense.

"In many ways, our process has evolved as we've learned more. Not only when it comes to interviewing and the hiring process, but also when it comes to the assimilation process and acclimating people into the new environment," Buckley shared.

He continued, "We've also learned that internal communication is important, and not just about what we're doing in terms of hiring these individuals with criminal convictions. You tell stories of individuals who have seen success. We've taken a risk on them, and we've given them a second chance. It's almost like a call to action. Internally, it gives people hope and stimulates ideas."

|||||||||||||||||||||||||||||||||

## Exercise

What did you find most surprising about the results of the SHRM and Koch Institute survey?

_____

_____

_____

_____

Which of the results would be most helpful if you were making a business case to your company's ownership/management about implementing second chance hiring?

_____

_____

_____

_____

# 6

# The Benefits of
# Second Chance Hiring

Employers need to shift their perspectives about second chance hiring. Many think it is about sacrificing profit to do good for individuals, but that is far from the truth. Second chance hiring is not — and should not be — about charity or handouts to applicants simply because they happen to have a criminal past.

Second chance hiring — like any process of bringing on a new worker — is about an equal exchange of value. Job seekers bring their qualifications for the job, their enthusiasm, and their desire for a better life. And these job seekers expect something in return—money, benefits, and opportunities to grow and advance their careers with your company or elsewhere.

And while it is certainly true that providing fair employment opportunities for individuals will help individuals, I would never recommend a company lower their workforce quality standards to do so.

Several compelling—and profit-related—reasons exist for businesses to seriously consider second chance hiring as a part of their ongoing strategy to address workforce needs.

**A deep pool of talent to choose from:** As mentioned earlier, a large and broad pool of people with criminal convictions who can help fill workforce needs exists. These candidates range from entry-level workers with little employment history to those with extensive work experience and educational backgrounds.

**Less competition:** Workers with criminal convictions are not as highly sought after. As a result, companies who are more inclusive in hiring will often have many candidates to choose from and less competition.

**Lower turnover:** In a report by the US Chamber of Commerce, several business case studies and work by researchers show that employees with criminal backgrounds stay longer in a position than employees without criminal records.[1] This is likely due to two main reasons: 1) applicants who have been denied opportunities in the past are grateful to have a foot in the door and eager to show their appreciation by being loyal to the employer; and 2) those employees with criminal backgrounds simply have fewer options elsewhere (see the previous bullet about less competition).

**A better, stronger workforce:** Having an effective second chance hiring policy means a company has made a commitment to hiring the best candidates, regardless of criminal background. This produces a highly qualified and productive workforce.

**An easy way to address diversity, equity, and inclusion (DEI):** It is well demonstrated that communities of color and lower-income populations have been disproportionately affected by the US criminal justice system. By having more inclusive hiring policies that include those with past criminal justice involvement, an employer will automatically address any DEI concerns it may have. Furthermore, when people think about diversity, the first thought is often about race and gender, but diversity of background is also immensely valuable, something that second chance hiring provides.

---

1   US Chamber of Commerce. "The Business Case for Criminal Justice Reform: Second Chance Hiring." https://www.uschamber.com/workforce/education/the-business-case-criminal-justice-reform-second-chance-hiring. Accessed February 1, 2023.

**Access to federal programs and tax benefits:** For employers with concerns about hiring those with criminal convictions, the US government provides the Federal Bonding Program, which provides no-cost and deductible-free fidelity bonds to employers who hire from this population.[2] These bonds protect against employee misconduct committed on or away from the worksite. For employers who may have concerns about losses from employees with criminal histories, this is a powerful incentive to "take a chance." Further, employers who hire certain classes of individuals with criminal records can qualify for up to $2,400 savings on their federal income tax liability through the Work Opportunity Tax Credit.[3]

**A stronger community:** Many studies have shown that lower unemployment (or higher employment, depending on how you state it) and higher workforce participation rates in an area lead to reductions in crime, poverty, and homelessness. Additionally, more people working leads to a greater tax base for an area to draw upon to fund services for the entire community. While these advantages may not be quantifiable, it's likely that companies in communities positively impacted by second chance hiring will also experience these benefits.

**Workers with diverse skill sets:** Employers often cite skills such as motivation, flexibility, communication, and creativity as important in a potential worker. And these are the exact skills people with criminal convictions have often had to display.

For example, Rob, one of the best salespeople I have ever met (and I've met a lot of them) is a former "community-based freelance pharmaceutical distributor," and did some prison time for it. After the completion

2    The Federal Bonding Program. https://bonds4jobs.com/. Accessed February 1, 2023.

3    Internal Revenue Service. "Work Opportunity Tax Credit." https://www.irs.gov/businesses/small-businesses-self-employed/work-opportunity-tax-credit. Accessed February 1, 2023.

of his sentence, he has used the same communication and negotiation skills that helped him in his previous life to succeed in his new one. Additionally, he learned how to work in an environment where things were changing quickly and also got some people management experience.

Employers who can effectively evaluate a candidate's past skills and have the vision for how they can help their company will reap immense benefits in the form of dedicated employees and the discovery of "diamonds in the rough."

I have been painstaking in my attempts to confine our discussion of second chance employment to business benefits to avoid leaning on the "warm and fuzzy feelings" that may also come from helping individuals put their lives back on track. Here is another major reason businesses should provide second chance employment opportunities: recidivism prevention.

Recidivism is "the tendency of a convicted criminal to reoffend." According to a study commissioned by the US Department of Justice, the number one predictor of re-offense is poverty.[4]

It makes sense that money pressures would presage recidivism. Every person has financial realities. We must all pay for food, clothing, shelter, and transportation. These pressures are magnified if we have children to provide for as well.

I fully believe, if given the opportunity to make an honest buck, most people will. And I also believe without the opportunity to make a living wage, many people with criminal pasts will return to what they know to survive.

---

4    US DOJ, Office of Justice Programs: "Poverty, State Capital, and Recidivism Among Women Offenders." https://www.ojp.gov/ncjrs/virtual-library/abstracts/poverty-state-capital-and-recidivism-among-women-offenders. Accessed February 1, 2023.

Further, this return to criminal activity has ripple effects that impose new costs on society. A 2018 study by the State of Illinois quantified the cost of a single episode of recidivism at more than $150,000.[5] A new victim—either an individual or a business—is created in the community, making people feel less safe and involving law enforcement. If a business is victimized, higher prices may be passed on to consumers, and taxpayer dollars are spent on police activity.

As a parole officer once said to me, "Employers need to decide if they want people showing up to work to get a paycheck or showing up at their house to steal their stereo."

Also, the offender goes back into the criminal justice system. In the US, there are significant costs to having an individual in the penal system. In my home state of Washington, it costs approximately $42,000 per year to house an inmate.[6] In addition to that cost, the individual no longer contributes to the tax base as they would if gainfully employed. Earlier, I mentioned how a full 75 percent of formerly incarcerated individuals will be unemployed one year after release. A study undertaken by the United States Sentencing Commission found that for individuals who find employment during the first year after release, the recidivism rate drops by almost 40 percent.[7]

5    Illinois Sentencing Advisory Council: "The High Cost of Recidivism 2018 Report." https://spac.illinois.gov/publications/cost-benefit-analysis/high-cost-of-recidivism-2018. Accessed February 1, 2023.

6    WA State Department of Corrections: "FY2019 Cost per Incarcerated Individual Per Day." https://www.doc.wa.gov/docs/publications/reports/200-AR001.pdf. Accessed February 1, 2023.

7    United States Sentencing Commission: "Measuring Recidivism: The Criminal History Computation of the Federal Sentencing Guidelines - May 2004." https://www.ussc.gov/sites/default/files/pdf/research-and-publications/research-publications/2004/200405_Recidivism_Criminal_History.pdf. Accessed February 1, 2023.

And finally, the person who has reoffended is now at a further disadvantage in employment. The more recently someone committed a crime, and the greater the number of crimes a person has committed, the less likely an employer will give them a chance, which starts the cycle over again.

Until more employers recognize the important role they play in improving conditions for society by implementing more inclusive hiring practices, this will continue to be a major issue.

## Second Chance Success Story: Kelly Services and Toyota America[8]

As stated earlier, more than one-fifth of the US population struggles to find quality employment due to restrictive background screening practices. By being more inclusive of individuals with a criminal record, companies can grow and meet increasing demands. Doing so is not only ethically correct but also a wise business strategy.

Toyota and Kelly Services acknowledged this opportunity seven years ago, forming a partnership to offer individuals with non-violent criminal records employment opportunities at Toyota's Kentucky manufacturing facility in Georgetown.

The duo initiated a program to employ individuals with nonviolent criminal backgrounds, especially when the offenses were unrelated to their job roles. They eliminated the extra layer of background checks and implemented Kelly's more personalized screening process. To further bolster this initiative, they cultivated Diversity, Equity, and Inclusion (DEI) strategies and engaged stakeholders like educators, policymakers, and community members with tours of their facility. Consequently, Toyota broadened its talent reservoir, addressed vital staffing requirements, and enhanced employee retention.

Kelly has since assessed more than 1,200 applicants with criminal histories for roles at Toyota, with 92 percent qualifying. Of these, 645 took temporary roles at Toyota, and 156 became permanent employees. This initiative enriched Toyota's talent base by 20 percent and remarkably reduced the turnover rate by 70 percent, reaching a record low of 3 percent per month. Furthermore, none of the "second chance" workers were dismissed due to behavior related to their past. This pro-

---

8    Kelly Services. "Equity in Action: How Toyota & Kelly Are Knocking Down Criminal History Barriers." https://www.kellyservices.com/global/about-us/equity-at-work/equity-at-work-articles/equity-in-action-how-toyota--kelly-are-knocking-down-criminal-history-barriers/. Accessed February 1, 2023.

gram also enhanced the plant's diversity by more than 8 percent and reduced time-to-fill for positions.

A Kelly survey revealed significant public backing for such initiatives:

- 71 percent believe that employers should revise policies that instantly dismiss candidates with minor, non-violent criminal records.

- 76 percent favor businesses actively working against discriminatory employment barriers.

- 81 percent opine that firms must address and rectify biased hiring practices.

Toyota and Kelly have illustrated the business merits of granting second chances. They now aspire to encourage other organizations to emulate their approach. This aspiration underpins Toyota's Social Innovation mission and motivated Kelly to launch the "Kelly 33 Second Chances Program."

"Kelly 33" is designed to link hiring managers with a valuable yet untapped talent pool seeking another shot at employment. Their experience in this realm has cemented their belief in the potential of these candidates. This segment of job-seekers is eager to work, offering businesses a prime opportunity to bolster their workforce, enhance retention, and increase profitability.

|||||||||||||||||||||||||||||||||||||

## Exercise

Which benefits of second chance hiring do you find the most compelling and why?

---

---

---

---

For your organization, which two or three benefits would be most important?

_____

_____

_____

_____

# 7

# A Simple Solution to Bias When Evaluating Second Chance Candidates

Companies can remove many of the barriers associated with second chance hiring and reap many of the benefits by remaining curious. As I mentioned, many states have "banned the box" and set guidelines for when an employer can ask about an applicant's criminal history. This change has allowed many people with past criminal justice involvement to make it to the first interview. The problem of bias in hiring has not disappeared, however, because there is another box that individuals have to battle: the box in people's minds that is filled with beliefs and preconceived notions about those with criminal records.

Some common ones include:

- People with criminal records can't be trusted.

- They must be bad people.

- They can't help our business.

- They can only be used for entry-level positions.

- They don't deserve a second chance.

- Hiring them will make our workplace more dangerous.

How can companies overcome these biases? By taking a more nuanced and human approach to hiring. Companies can make better decisions and build better workforces by getting curious about applicants.

From a job seeker's perspective, looking for employment with a criminal record looks much the same regardless of which part of the US you are in. In my personal experience and based on stories shared by hundreds of others with criminal convictions, the experiences sound remarkably similar:

"I was lucky enough to get an interview, which went pretty well. They seemed to like my qualifications and I think they liked me as a person. All was going fine and it looked like they were going to make an offer, and they said all I had to do was finish the rest of the hiring process, which included a background check.

"And that's when everything changed. After they saw my background, the entire conversation was different. We weren't talking about my qualifications, or that funny thing I said in the interview, or how they thought I'd be a good fit. It was all about my past, and who I am today didn't seem to matter anymore."

Regardless of qualifications, culture, or job fit, when employers focus entirely on the criminal record, even if the candidate is the best applicant for the position, the entire tenor of the hiring process transforms.

If the employer were simply to slow down and get curious about the applicant's story, the company might find a viable candidate who should be given an opportunity.

I'm not suggesting the employer ask anything that might put them in legal jeopardy. Employers already sufficiently make the first inquiry by asking something like: "Would you please explain the circumstances of your conviction(s)?"

While this question allows the candidate to provide context (a good thing), the problem with it (and with background checks in general) is it is a backward-looking inquiry. It focuses on who the candidate used to be and tells you nothing about the person you are speaking with on the phone, on Zoom, or who might be sitting across from you in a conference room. It is certainly possible that the applicant has made no changes and could be the same person who picked up the criminal conviction(s), but how would you know if this question is the only one you ask?

Employers rarely ask the second question, which I believe is much more valuable: "What's been happening since your last conviction?"

My advice is to shut up, listen, and observe a few things:

- Did the candidate tell you before you ran the background check that you would find convictions? If so, this is a sign of integrity and honesty—good qualities for a potential employee.

- When the applicant explained the circumstances of their previous life, did they take responsibility or blame others? Accountability is a highly desirable trait in an employee.

- Is it clear by their activities that they are making an effort to live a different life? This is truly a sign that the applicant is worth consideration.

- Can they provide references or documentation supporting what they tell you? If someone else had a positive experience with this applicant that you can verify, that is the best sign of all!

What does living a "different life" look like? It could be any number of things.

Remember back in the introduction when I told my story about being homeless and addicted and my criminal convictions? Almost any employer would have hesitated to hire me if I was still living my life that way.

After I had been in recovery for about a year, I was referred by a counselor to a small manufacturing company for my first really good opportunity, meaning I was qualified, had a real shot at getting hired, and it fit my advanced skills. It was for an outside sales position doing business development, a job I was probably overqualified for based on my education and work history. However, I took the interview because I was desperate for a chance.

Today, due to the pandemic, it is common for an HR professional or hiring manager to see a resume with a two- or three-year job gap. But in 2017 when I interviewed, a gap of that size was a major red flag. On top of that, I had reason to be nervous. The part of my recovery journey back to employment I didn't share in the introduction is I had many interviews that did not result in employment. Despite being lucky in education, employment, and interviewing skills, I was repeatedly told I was not eligible for hire due to my misdemeanor convictions. I was even denied positions by companies who told me in the interview I was the best and most qualified, even when the work was completely unrelated to the crimes I had been convicted of.

As a result, the only job I could get was part-time as a janitor.

Don't get me wrong. Janitorial, cleaning, housekeeping, and custodial work are honorable and necessary professions. I was simply surprised at how limited my options were.

Therefore, although I was absolutely qualified for this prospective position at the small manufacturer, I was also nervous based on past experiences. But this interview was different because they took the time to ask me not only about my job gap but what had been going on in my life since my last job.

And did I have a story to tell! In my interview, I pointed to several things that showed I was trying to live a different life. I had:

- Entered a Twelve-Step program and worked with a sponsor whose name and phone number I offered to provide.

- Volunteered many hours at a local food bank and supplied a letter of recommendation from my supervisor there.

- Worked part time for about a year as a janitor and had a recommendation letter from the owner of the company.

- Joined a church.

- Reconnected with my friends and family, who were offering me great support.

All this made it clear I wasn't the same person who had been addicted, homeless, and convicted of multiple crimes. But they only knew about these aspects of my life because they took the time to get curious and ask the question.

I got that job and stayed there for three years until I moved on to my current field. And more importantly, according to that small manufacturer, I was a great contributor during my time there.

If you open your company up to second chance hiring, you may sometimes encounter job seekers who served many years in prison. For some candidates, this experience was the catalyst for changing their lives. When considering those applicants, you should take a look at what they did while incarcerated. Did they:

- Get a diploma or degree?

- Learn job skills?

- Participate in counseling or anger management classes?

- Engage in recovery-related activities?

Also, were they able to provide a letter of recommendation from their parole or probation officer?

These are indications an applicant may be qualified and ready for the opportunity you have to offer. And don't forget, you can offset some of the risks by using the federal bonding program mentioned earlier.

It takes courage to overcome poor decisions and unfortunate circum-stances. At the very least, people who demonstrate that courage deserve the opportunity to show they are indeed moving in the right direction. And they will never get that opportunity if employers don't slow down, get curious, and give them an honest evaluation.

## Second Chance Success Story: Pioneer Human Services

Seattle, Washington, is home to Pioneer Human Services, a social enterprise that's making a difference in the lives of individuals transitioning from incarceration and addiction. Guided by its COO Mark Behrends, the organization is dedicated to providing a much-needed second chance.

Behrends describes their mission succinctly, "Our mission is to give those that are coming out of incarceration and addiction a second chance. We do that through a number of programs we offer in employment, housing, treatment, or skill development and training."

Beyond offering a comprehensive range of services, Pioneer has a strong focus on preparing their clients for employment. As part of this process, confidence and self-esteem building are key, enabling clients to face job interviews and potential employers with a renewed sense of self-belief and a positive attitude.

Pioneer's commitment to its clients doesn't end when they secure a job. Recognizing the critical first year post-incarceration or recovery from addiction as the most challenging, the organization offers case management support for up to nine months after an individual starts employment.

For employers who might be skeptical about hiring people with criminal records, Behrends advises open-mindedness. He emphasizes that people who have been given a second chance often show a higher level of appreciation for their opportunities and have a strong commitment to avoid reverting to old ways. Behrends also acknowledges the presence of societal bias against individuals with criminal records. He believes that recognizing and addressing these biases is crucial to integrating these individuals back into the workforce.

Discussing his personal inspiration, Behrends shares, "It's very inspiring to me to see the success and the hard work and attention to detail in their lives. The scars are never gone, but they can be managed."

With two-thirds of their internal employees coming from criminal justice backgrounds, Pioneer Human Services shines a light on the transformative power of redemption and the potential that lies within each person. It's not just an organization that helps reintegrate individuals into society; it's a symbol of hope.

||||||||||||||||||||||||||||||||||||||

## Exercise

What policies does your company have in place for evaluating candidates with criminal convictions?

_____

_____

_____

_____

What could a candidate present to convince you they are living their lives "the right way"?

_____

_____

_____

_____

# 8

# Is Second Chance Hiring Right for Your Company?

Although I genuinely believe second chance hiring is the answer to many of the problems employers have with recruiting, I also acknowledge there are often significant internal hurdles for businesses to overcome and questions to answer before adopting new policies. Those questions include:

- What criminal backgrounds will we accept?

- Where do we find the talent?

- What are the risks if we do this? How do we mitigate these?

- Does the potential to gain outweigh those risks?

- What is our responsibility to our existing workforce? Our ownership/shareholders? The community?

- How do we balance equity with maintaining a safe working environment?

- How do we avoid getting sued?

- How do we construct new policies so we won't get accused of favoring one group over another (also called disparate treatment)?

- How do we overcome the bias of some HR and hiring managers about people with criminal records?

These are all valid questions and concerns. I believe employers can do three things to address many of these issues, protect themselves legally, and provide a fair opportunity for those who deserve it. Those three things are:

1. **Learn about and dedicate your company to following the EEOC guidance on how to evaluate these candidates:** In the policy guidance mentioned previously, the EEOC recommends that employers consider three main things when assessing those with criminal convictions.

   • The nature of the crime

   • The time elapsed since the conviction

   • The nature of the position

   This is an excellent starting point and framework. It provides protection for a company to, for example, avoid hiring a recent embezzler for an accounting position. It also leaves room to consider that same embezzler if they are qualified for an unrelated position.

2. **Place more emphasis on the candidate's qualifications for the position:** Under the current systems most companies use, even if the applicant is highly qualified, emphasis is placed on their criminal background once it is discovered. When a candidate is qualified, and you like the candidate, try to keep liking them by getting curious about their current life. If they provide supporting evidence, be open to giving them a chance.

3. **Communicate your dedication to offering fair employment opportunities to job seekers, your employees, and customers:** Many companies have an EEOC statement that is something like:

   ABC Company provides equal employment opportunities to all employees and applicants for employment and prohibits discrimination and harassment of any type without regard to race, color, religion, age, sex, national origin, disability status, genetics, protected veteran status, sexual orientation, gender identity or expression, or any other characteristic protected by federal, state, or local laws.

This can be made more powerful and inclusive by adding just a few words:

ABC Company provides equal employment opportunities to all employees and applicants for employment and prohibits discrimination and harassment of any type without regard to race, color, religion, age, sex, national origin, disability status, genetics, protected veteran status, sexual orientation, gender identity or expression, ***unrelated criminal history***, or any other characteristic protected by federal, state, or local laws.

These three additional words send a message to the community, your employees, and prospective applicants that your company cares about providing opportunities for qualified applicants who deserve them.

In many ways, these suggestions provide support for the process HR professionals and hiring managers already use when hiring for any position. They look at a resume, how well the candidate interviewed, and attempt to evaluate these and other factors without bias to decide whether an applicant is the right fit for the advertised position. Depending on the employer's needs, if HR/hiring managers believe a candidate can bring value to the organization but is not a fit for the position for which they applied, they may suggest another current or soon-to-be available position. All that is required to extend this process to second chance employment candidates is the curiosity mentioned earlier. By asking questions, we open ourselves to overcoming our biases and providing opportunities to candidates who desperately need them.

## Second Chance Success Story: CKS Packaging[1]

CKS Packaging, a family-owned business with twenty-four nationwide plants, initiated the Second Chance Program in 2016. The program aims to provide employment opportunities to people facing challenges in the job market such as ex-convicts, the homeless, and those recovering from drug addictions. This initiative has been successful in offering hundreds of people a fresh start and reducing the strain on taxpayer-funded social support systems.

CKS Packaging collaborates with community organizations to find suitable candidates for this program. Since its establishment, the Second Chance Program has been highly beneficial, providing a dedicated and hard-working workforce for the company. Additionally, it has fostered social and financial independence among its participants, disrupting cycles of poverty, crime, and addiction.

The societal benefits of this initiative could have significant implications if replicated by other businesses. It helps to alleviate the major challenges faced by previously incarcerated people, including unemployment, heavy debt, lack of supportive resources, and the stigma of a criminal record. All these issues contribute to a high re-arrest rate.

Georgia, a state with a notably high incarceration rate, has greatly benefited from the Second Chance Program. More than 5 percent of adults in Georgia are under the supervision of the criminal justice system. This scenario places a massive financial burden on taxpayers because the costs associated with prisons, welfare, and supportive services are high.

---

1    https://foropportunity.org/wp-content/uploads/2020/08/THE-SECOND-CHANCE-PROGRAM-AT-CKS-PACKAGING.pdf. Accessed July 19, 2023.

The Prisoner Reentry Initiative of the Georgia Center for Opportunity, established in 2013, strives to overcome these barriers. By urging employers to provide opportunities to individuals reintegrating into society, it promotes the establishment of "Second Chance" programs.

CKS Packaging, headquartered in Atlanta, has been a prominent advocate for this cause. Its long-standing tradition of hiring marginalized individuals aligns with the company's Christian-based principles of supporting those in need.

In 2016, the company formalized its employment efforts for marginalized individuals through the introduction of the Second Chance Program. The program began in Atlanta, partnering with local service organizations for worker referrals. It then expanded to five other regions where CKS Packaging has plants, employing 183 people in six locations across the United States.

The program has positively impacted both CKS Packaging and its employees. It has enabled hundreds of participants to secure stable jobs, learn necessary skills, and achieve financial independence. Of the 473 individuals employed since the program's inception, 39 percent remain employed within the program, while 25 percent have moved on to better positions with other companies.

These success rates are noteworthy, given that two-thirds of formerly incarcerated people face rearrest within three years of release, and 85 percent of individuals relapse post-drug addiction treatment. The program has also seen some of its employees rise to supervisory or managerial levels.

CKS Packaging's Second Chance Program exemplifies the potential of corporate social responsibility in tackling societal issues while benefiting the company itself. The company hopes that its success will inspire other businesses to adopt similar initiatives.

## Exercise

Which owners, managers, or stakeholders at your company would be most likely to support policies in favor of providing more opportunity to applicants with criminal convictions? How can you garner more of their support?

_____

_____

_____

_____

Which owners, managers, or stakeholders at your company would offer resistance? What information will you need to provide to begin to address their concerns?

_____

_____

_____

_____

# 9

# The Risks of Second Chance Hiring

While I am an obvious proponent of hiring those with criminal records because of the difference it has made in the lives of many (including mine), this book would be incomplete if I didn't speak to the risks attached to second chance hiring.

Several risks exist, although not all of these are exclusive to second chance hiring. Below are the three most prevalent risks.

**Negligent hiring:** While employers often state this is the biggest risk, there are some easy ways to mitigate the risk of being sued for negligence. Background checks combined with a fair and equitable hiring process for applicants with criminal justice histories are an effective way to combat the risk of litigation due to negligence. While I do not like the way employers use background checks in the hiring process, I do not oppose their use overall.

Some industries have hiring standards dictated by industry or government guidelines, such as positions where an applicant will be in charge of vulnerable populations. For the most part, however, many employers across different industries can feel confident they will be shielded from the possibility of a negligent hiring lawsuit with proper due diligence.

**A poor evaluation process can lead to poor hires:** When I speak to groups of employers or human resources people, someone will often say something like, "We hired a couple of people with criminal records, and it was a disaster."

My immediate response is to thank them for being open to providing an opportunity for someone who probably genuinely needed it. But then I quickly ask them what process they used.

Often, the answer is something like, "We do it on a case-by-case basis."

I have a strong bias against this response for a number of reasons. Granted, in some rare instances, saying "case-by-case" can have meaning if the company is adhering to the EEOC standard for using "individualized assessments" when working with applicants with previous criminal justice involvement. Still, mostly that is not what is happening. "Case-by-case" often means something entirely different—and dangerous—for an organization.

First of all, saying your company evaluates these candidates on a case-by-case basis means nothing. Every candidate — regardless of criminal history — is judged on a case-by-case basis using their resume, how they interview, and their perceived fit within your company's culture.

Second, saying it is case-by-case tells me a company doesn't have a formal process for evaluating these applicants. Often, that means someone went with their "gut" in making a hiring decision (positively or negatively) or went by some other factor (like communication style) in making the hire.

Finally, using the case-by-case method provides a company with absolutely no protection against lawsuits for discriminatory hiring practices. As I mentioned in the introduction, poorly designed hiring practices that are used to exclude applicants with criminal justice system involvement can expose a company to complaints of discrimination. Responding to EEOC and human rights commission complaints and lawsuits is distracting for the business and expensive even if the business wins.

Almost all this risk can be avoided by establishing a defined process for evaluating second chance candidates. (I'll discuss this in more detail in the upcoming "How To" section.)

**The employee may not have fully left behind their old life:** This is the hardest risk factor for an employer to judge. Often, recovery from a rocky past is not a straight line and there are bumps along the way. I know many people (including me) who have started down the path to recovery and then suffered a setback of some sort.

These setbacks don't necessarily mean the person isn't still committed to recovery and their new life. They also don't mean the person cannot be a good employee long-term. In these cases, what is most important is what they do next.

- Do they redouble their efforts and commit more fully to their new path?

- Do they examine what led them to temporarily return to their old ways?

- Do they seek help or isolate themselves from the support they need?

An employer asking about candidates' new lives and securing supporting documentation is a great way to perform due diligence and can provide reassurance about the hiring decision, thereby lowering possible risk. What can never be accounted for while hiring from this or any population is human nature.

Thus far, I have presented what I hope is compelling enough information to impress upon employers why they should make second chance hiring part of their overall recruitment efforts. In the next section, I will explain how this can be done with relatively low risk while still attracting good candidates.

# Second Chance Success Story: Next Chapter, a Nonprofit

Despite decades-long societal and systemic barriers, a non-profit organization is tackling the significant issue of ex-offender reintegration into the workforce. Led by Kenyatta Leal, the Next Chapter organization is demonstrating the power of second chances and challenging common misconceptions about individuals with criminal records.

Next Chapter is an eight-month apprenticeship program offering career paths in software engineering for formerly incarcerated individuals. Articulating the organization's vision, Leal states, "Our mission is to foster a more equitable workplace for people who are formerly incarcerated," a crucial step in helping them reintegrate into society and reclaim control of their lives.

This initiative fills a gap in the societal structure by providing much-needed support and guidance to a marginalized population. Next Chapter's approach is grounded in open communication, understanding, and patience, providing a platform for individuals to express their concerns and ambitions without fear of judgment or dismissal. The organization extends support beyond employment, helping these individuals navigate personal development, goal-setting, and other life skills.

Although Next Chapter has been operational since 2018 and boasts a zero recidivism rate among its nearly fifty graduates, Leal emphasizes that this is only the beginning. "While these figures are promising, they represent just the tip of the iceberg in tackling the widespread issue of reintegration faced by our country," he cautions.

For Leal, the change in perspective and approach toward individuals with criminal records needs to be society-wide. His outlook is clear: "We've come up with a thousand ways to make sure a plastic bottle or an aluminum can gets a new life but far too few to make sure that somebody getting out of prison does." This call for systemic change goes beyond mere tolerance to recognizing the value in people and their potential to contribute meaningfully to society and the economy.

The importance of such initiatives can't be overstated, especially considering the numerous roadblocks that formerly incarcerated individuals face upon reentry into society. Leal, a formerly incarcerated individual himself, states, "Not everyone has a bank account or a family that they can fall back on. People need help. They need support." His lived experiences fuel his passion and drive to foster change, challenge stereotypes, and influence societal attitudes.

Next Chapter is more than an organization; it's an embodiment of redemption, change, and hope. It's a testament to how with the right resources and support, people can change their lives, contribute to society, and break the cycle of recidivism. As Leal passionately posits, "I believe we each have a responsibility to understand and act upon our role in the community, shaping it into a welcoming place for those reentering from incarceration."

|||||||||||||||||||||||||||||||||||||

## Exercise

What do you feel is the greatest risk in second chance hiring for your company? Why?

_____

_____

_____

_____

What steps can you take to mitigate some of this risk? Who within your company could you partner with to determine how to make the risks acceptable?

_____

_____

_____

_____

# 10

# The How: Low, Medium, and High Effort Ways to Implement Second Chance Hiring in Your Organization

As you have been reading this book, I hope you have been thinking about how you might implement second chance hiring within your organization. Some readers may have already begun considering who they will need to convince within their companies to put more inclusive hiring practices in place. The great news is you don't have to implement these changes all at once, and there are easy ways to increase opportunities for those with criminal convictions without making huge changes to what you do currently.

When I work with organizations intrigued by the thought of second chance hiring but wary of making a huge commitment, I encourage them to use what I call "the 10 percent strategy." This is the concept of taking existing policies and "nibbling" around the edges to open up opportunities for your company to benefit from a broader pool of workers and job seekers.

For companies who currently do not hire applicants with past criminal convictions, the perception may exist that implementing a second chance hiring strategy is a radical departure from how they currently do business. However, there is a lot of room between disregarding job seekers with conviction histories and accepting every qualified applicant regardless of background.

Consider these "10 percent strategy" methods of creating additional opportunities without radical change to current practices and policies. If you currently do not:

- **Accept any applicants with criminal convictions**—implement a policy that states you will disregard unrelated misdemeanors in the last three years.

- **Hire people with any crimes in the last five or seven years**—lower that number to three or five years (or less).

- **Consider the nature of the crime committed**—write a policy that allows for some low-level, nonviolent offenses unrelated to the job offered for qualified applicants.

During my consulting work with companies nervous about fully diving into second chance hiring, we focus on the above areas. While the suggestions may seem like small things, they create additional opportunities for those who deserve and need them while not placing a great burden on the organization.

In addition to these 10 percent moves, organizations can decide how much effort they want to put into second chance hiring. In the following passage, I'll describe some low, medium, and high-effort strategies to implement within your company.

To me, the difference between a low, medium, or high-effort strategy is:

- **Low**—little effort to implement or the bare minimum legally. This effort will require little in the way of time or resources. It is easy to implement, but also will not realize many of the possible benefits of second chance hiring. The more effort an organization puts in, the more attractive applicants it will attract.

- **Medium**—takes the low-effort actions into consideration and adds layers of a couple of more advanced concepts. Medium effort will mean changing some of your internal documentation and possibly your website. You may also need to implement some additional policies and procedures.

- **High**—includes the low and medium efforts. The high effort area adds more investigation and amending of current positions, building partnerships with outside, community-based organizations, and consulting with professionals who work in the area of second chance hiring to assist your company in making these changes. For organizations that wish to really make second chance hiring a significant part of their overall hiring strategy, these high-effort steps will make a huge difference in your business and impact the quality and number of job seekers you attract.

Let me now provide you with some examples of how you can make low, medium, or high effort changes to implement second chance hiring in your organization.

## Low Effort

**Use the EEOC guidance on how to evaluate these candidates:** I call this a low-effort method because all it requires is following the law (although for some employers with significant bias against criminally involved populations, that could be a tough ask). Read the guidance, look at the nature of the crime and how much time has passed since it occurred, and carefully evaluate whether the position the applicant is applying for is related to the crime(s) they committed.

**Fairly consider job seekers through the natural flow of applications:** You don't have to go find these applicants somewhere. As you interview candidates, job seekers who need a second chance will find you. Remember, there are tens of millions of us in America!

In larger organizations, only the HR department will know what is on the applicant's background check, but for smaller companies where the hiring manager may know as well, have you had training or communication with that manager to ensure they are using an unbiased approach? If not, you should build a simple process that works to eliminate bias as much as possible. Helpful tools include using a standard scorecard and panel interviews with at least two people (An example of what to put in a scorecard is provided on pages 90 to 92).

SHRM also has some excellent tools on its website at SHRM.org that can help remove bias from the hiring process.

## Medium Effort

**Add a blurb to your EEOC statement in your job postings, employee handbook, and website:** As mentioned previously, add the simple phrase "and unrelated criminal offenses" to the end of your EEOC statement regarding your company's commitment to fair and inclusive hiring practices.

In addition to signaling the community and your stakeholders about your organization's desire to inject equity into the hiring process, there is a major added benefit: You will get many more applicants to choose from. As with any other source of job candidates, not all of them will be qualified or fit your culture, but the important part is you'll be seeing many more applications, which in today's tight labor market has been a major issue.

**Internally publish your disqualifying offenses for criminal history and share those policies with applicants before performing preemployment background checks:** I don't understand why more companies don't do this.

Actually, that's not true. I know why companies don't do this. Not having clearly communicated guidelines around which offenses might get someone disqualified from consideration gives an organization the wiggle room to turn people down for any number of biases the business might have against a particular group while hoping to avoid litigation. In my mind, that is not very ethical.

Having opaque policies around why and how people with challenged backgrounds will not be hired is a huge waste of time for both the company and the job seeker. Plus, if an organization simply follows the EEOC rules, it can easily justify why it didn't hire an individual if their background is inconsistent with the job requirements.

By creating clarity internally for HR employees and hiring managers, and by sharing these policies with applicants, companies can save time and money, and avoid frustrating job seekers.

## High Effort

**Analyze every position in your company to seek opportunities for those with criminal convictions:** No law says that all positions in your business must have the same background check requirements, and it isn't even practical for them to. Why should the warehouse person have the same background check as your accountant?

Inspect categories or individual positions (depending on your company's size), and carefully consider what type of screening process makes sense. In positions where there is no contact with vulnerable populations, or where there is no access to significant company funds, a lowered risk exists, which should be taken into consideration when evaluating job seekers.

This evaluation process is a part of the "10 percent strategy" mentioned earlier. New opportunities can easily be created with relatively little risk if you can tweak the screening process and background requirements for warehouse, labor, sales, or customer service positions.

**Establish relationships with community-based organizations and government agencies that serve those with criminal convictions:** Establishing such relationships will allow you to create a pipeline of mutual support. This effort requires some research and networking but will pay huge dividends for your organization.

In almost every community, nonprofits exist that specialize in providing social assistance, job training, and placement services for people with barriers to employment, such as past addiction, homelessness, and criminal justice involvement. These nonprofits always seek relationships with employers.

Many advantages result from connecting with these organizations. The main one is they produce job seekers who are trained and eager to work. You are plugging into a pipeline of potential employees by partnering with these community-based organizations.

Since many nonprofit organizations receive compensation from the federal or state government in return for training and placing their job candidates, employers receive services at no cost. (I never say "free" because your business is receiving services that are funded by tax dollars you have already paid into the system.)

Some government agencies also provide some of these same services. American Job Centers[1] are located in every state to help job seekers find work. The Rehabilitation Services Administration,[2] while technically established to help people with disabilities become job ready, provides services for a wide range of job seekers. They often serve individuals who have been in the criminal justice system or were formerly in active addiction. (Addiction is considered a disability by the US government.)

And while your company can partner with any of these nonprofits or government agencies for no cost, there is one other major advantage to adding these organizations to your hiring toolbox: They continue to

---

1     American Job Centers. https://www.careeronestop.org/localhelp/americanjob-centers/find-american-job-centers.aspx. Accessed February 1, 2023.

2     Rehabilitation Services Administration. https://rsa.ed.gov/about/states. Accessed February 1, 2023.

support the job seeker after they are placed for employment with your company.

Besides being compensated for training and placing job seekers into employment, these nonprofits or government agencies also receive significant revenue from ensuring the employee is retained. As a result, they stay in contact with you and the job seeker for a period of anywhere from three to twelve months.

That means your company gets a de facto "shadow HR" representative, whose main concern is keeping the new employee on the job. And this shadow HR (SHR) person can ask many questions you can't.

For example, let's say you hire Johnny from the local nonprofit after he completes work readiness training, and he starts out as a great employee for the first sixty days. But then, things start to change. Johnny starts showing up late, and his work quality declines.

Johnny's front-line manager can ask if he can help and offer solutions, but he can't get to the heart of the problem due to privacy laws. But the SHR rep can. Since the nonprofit organization helped Johnny get work-ready, they had to know about all of Johnny's barriers to holding employment so they could help him deal with them.

So, the SHR can ask Johnny if he relapsed and offer treatment options. They can ask if his car broke down or if his "baby mama" is causing drama in his life and making things difficult. The SHR can deal with all the stuff in Johnny's life outside of work that impacts how he shows up to work.

Partnering with these nonprofit organizations or government agencies provides support for you and the employee and is a win-win-win scenario.

**Engage a second chance hiring consultant to determine which of your policies are screening out people and instead seek to screen in people:** Not only can a consultant help your company with all of the above but they can also help with a review of your current policies so you can work through the amendment process to make them more inclusive.

A consultant can also assist in a variety of other areas:

- Discovering workforce development programs and grants in your city and state

- Researching sources of workers in your local community

- Applying for Work Opportunity Tax Credits

- Establishing relationships with parole and probation officers and sober houses, making it easier to find candidates

- Helping you establish an internal peer-mentor program to help new hires

And possibly more depending on your company's needs.

**Implement a specific scorecard to evaluate candidates with criminal backgrounds:** Using a scorecard that takes into account the additional information needed to assess candidates from this pool does three crucial things:

- Removes the possible bias that can be infused into the hiring process when evaluating these applicants.

- Protects the company—if anyone ever files a lawsuit claiming they were discriminated against, the scorecard provides documentation that a formal process was explicitly used to remove bias from the process.

- Allows the company to determine what information they need to learn to feel secure in hiring an applicant with criminal justice history.

The proposed model has several questions that could be supplied to or asked of an applicant with criminal convictions. The company could then assign value to the information they receive to determine if a candidate is eligible for hire. For example, a company could have a scorecard that uses a 100-point scale; if a prospective employee scores 80 or better, they would be eligible for hire. Scores below 80 would indicate the applicant is not eligible for hire today, but if the information changes, they may be in the future. For example, if the candidate's latest conviction was a year ago, which leads to a lower score, they may be eligible for hire if they come back a year from today or if they gain more work experience, leading to a higher score.

Here are some possible things to include in a scorecard to evaluate candidates with criminal convictions:

- Are the applicant's convictions related to the position for which they are applying?*

- How long ago did the crime occur?*

- Has the candidate had volunteer or work experience since the last offense?**

- If yes, how much experience?**

- Has the applicant enrolled in or completed any employment-related training or additional education since their last offense?

- Was the applicant referred to us by a current or former employee (in good standing with the organization)?

- Did a community-based organization refer the applicant? Will this organization provide job retention support?

- Does the applicant have other community or social supports?

- Has the applicant provided letters of recommendation or reference contact information?

*Note: These items can probably be evaluated by simply looking at the criminal background check results.

**Note: These items may be apparent on the applicant's resume.

For more answers about how this model could work within your company, please check the blogs on my website at recoveryandwork.org, or reach out to me directly using the contact information at the end of the book.

No matter what approach you take, almost every company can benefit from taking some action to address hiring practices. Even if you decide not to make any changes after starting down the path and analyzing your current state, the awareness you'll gain from having done a close inspection of your policies and procedures is priceless.

## Second Chance Success Story: Freymiller Trucking[3]

At Freymiller Trucking, the guiding principle is the impact made on others, a principle brilliantly embodied in their Second Chance Program. This joint initiative with the Oklahoma Department of Corrections, Career Tech, and Central Tech Truck Driving School, focuses on equipping former felons with skills to become professional truck drivers.

The Second Chance Program was the brainchild of Freymiller's CEO, David Freymiller, conceived as a means of giving back to Oklahoma, the state that had supported their business. Though initially overwhelmed by the enormity of the task, Betsy Waldrop, Freymiller's Recruiting and Training director, connected with the right resources to bring the program to life.

John Thorpe, director of Central Tech Truck Driving School, explains how their prior attempts to initiate a similar program faced obstacles. However, with Freymiller's commitment to hiring newly released individuals, they breathed life into the endeavor. The unique aspect of Freymiller's program is the immediate employment opportunity it offers to released individuals, irrespective of the age of their convictions.

The candidates undergo a thorough vetting process, focusing on their commitment to sobriety, maturity, safety, and readiness to start afresh. Barrett Richardson, project manager for Career Tech, works closely with probation officers and counselors during the vetting process. Despite the process being time-consuming and allowing for potential setbacks, the emphasis remains on the program being a second chance—no third chances are given.

---

3    Truck Drivers US. "Freymiller Sets the Standard for Fair Chance Hiring With Second Chance Program." https://truckdriversus.com/freymiller-sets-the-stan-dard-for-fair-chance-hiring-with-second-chance-program/. Accessed February 1, 2023.

Once accepted, candidates complete a rigorous twenty-eight-day training program at Central Tech, learning everything necessary to be professional drivers. Waldrop maintains that these candidates start with a clean slate and are treated like any other student.

Since its initiation, the Second Chance Program has significantly impacted the lives of its graduates. Many of the hundreds who have graduated are now gainfully employed, some at Freymiller, and some have even started their families. The success of this program is changing lives and influencing other states to consider similar initiatives.

The impact of this program, however, goes beyond mere numbers. It is about empowering individuals to reintegrate into society and rebuild their lives with dignity. Richardson sums it up best, saying, "With this second chance program with Freymiller, these guys can be making $70-$90k a year or more. It's a career. It's life changing money." The Second Chance Program proves that the road to redemption begins with a single step—or in this case, a single drive.

||||||||||||||||||||||||||||||||||||

## Exercise

Look back at the list of efforts your company can make. Which ones seem most realistic for your organization?

_____

_____

_____

_____

How can you implement at least one of these ideas in the next ninety days? Will you commit to implementing a second or third effort in the next 180 days? If so, how can you accomplish this?

_____

_____

_____

_____

# A Final Note

I hope this short book has given you some things to consider as you inspect your overall hiring strategy. Companies today need to be creative, flexible, and open-minded about finding the best talent. Second chance hiring should be a part of your strategy.

In addition to the work I do with companies to help them determine whether second chance hiring fits into their overall strategy, I also speak on this topic and about how companies can create recovery-friendly workplaces (the two subjects are often intertwined).

Quite often after I speak to an audience, someone will approach me to tell me they don't have hire and fire authority at their company, but they see the value in helping this pool of job seekers. They want to know what they can do to assist someone with criminal convictions who is attempting to change their lives.

It's simple: advocate.

And when I say that, I'm not talking about to going to your state capitol and lobbying legislators (although we need people to do that, too). What I mean is if you see someone who is working to overcome barriers and seems to be on the right path, help them as best you can. Maybe you could:

- Take the time to learn a bit about their story. Get curious, just like I encourage HR people and hiring managers to do. That way you know whom you're advocating for.

- Keep an eye out at your company for positions that may be right for them, and try to get them an interview. It's their responsibility to show up and impress at the interview, but getting their foot in the door can be key.

- If someone in your network has an appropriate position, do the same.

- Encourage, encourage, encourage the individual to stay focused on the process, even when it gets tough—and it will.

For every comeback story we see in movies, on TV, or in books, after our hero begins the part of their journey where they go through pain, learn, and then change, there is always a person or group of people who "magically" appear to help them take the next step. You can be that person for someone you haven't even met yet. What a great experience for you and whomever this stranger is!

If you have any questions about the content of this book or want to determine whether hiring from this pool of extremely talented individuals is right for you, let's connect. I've provided several ways on the last page of this book.

Good luck on your hiring and recruiting journey!

Ty Reed
Second Chance Coach and Consultant
Recovery Career Services

# About the Author

TY REED is an author, professional keynote speaker, career and recovery coach, and workforce development and human resources consultant.

Ty was inspired by his own struggles with addiction, homelessness, and criminal convictions to help others walk the road to redemption. He thought the best way to do that was to be vulnerable and tell his story, and he proudly and openly lives as a person in recovery to show others that change is truly possible.

As a career and recovery coach, Ty has been able to help dozens of individuals with criminal convictions find and keep work. As a workforce development and human resources consultant, he has spoken to hundreds of companies about their hiring practices and provided practical advice on becoming more inclusive. As a professional keynote speaker, Ty has been featured in magazines and podcasts and presented to thousands of human resources practitioners, business owners and association members, front-line managers, and C-Suite executives who have enjoyed Ty's mix of humor, practical advice, and storytelling.

Ty holds many professional designations and educational achievements, including a Master's in Business Administration from the Foster School of Business at the University of Washington, a Professional in Human Resources (PHR) designation from HRCI, a Certified Workforce Development Professional (CWDP) credential from the National

Association of Workforce Development Professionals, and a Certified Facilitator of Addiction Awareness in Human Resources (CFAA-HR). He is also a Certified Peer Counselor in his home state of Washington. He was recently named one of the top fifteen coaches in Seattle by *Influence Digest*.

Born in the same small town outside of Memphis, Tennessee, as his parents, Ty has lived in many different states and now currently resides outside of Seattle, Washington, where he keeps a busy schedule of speaking, consulting, coaching, playing pickleball, and singing karaoke.

# About Ty Reed Coaching

If you are serious about helping your employees be their best at home and in the workplace, demonstrating your commitment to treating employees with compassion, and increasing retention, then the **Reclaim My Career** program is the answer.

Often, employees who struggle with substance issues are overlooked, even though they still have value to bring to the company. Companies usually have Employee Assistance Programs (EAPs) and insurance that will pay for employees to attend treatment, but once they return to the office, no formal support exists to help them with what can be an overwhelming transition.

The **Reclaim My Career** program is the best option to provide professional recovery coaching to your employees. It is tightly focused on their recovery and helping them be better employees. This confidential, customized program will show participants how to:

- Prepare for their return to the company

- Manage their new journey in recovery and become better employees

- Improve communications with their supervisors and coworkers

- Rebuild lost trust and enhance their reputation in the workplace

Don't feel lost in how to best care for this important group of workers while balancing your business' needs. Let author, professional keynote speaker, career and recovery coach, and workforce development and human resources consultant Ty Reed help you overcome these challenges.

For more information, please visit Ty's website and then text him your name, time zone, and the best time for you to redeem a 30- to 60-minute, no-obligation, complimentary consultation by phone or Zoom.

https://www.RecoveryAndWork.org/Reclaim-My-Career

(253) 347-1611

# About Ty Reed
# Employer Consulting

Ty Reed offers consulting to employers facing difficult situations, such as second chance hiring, and formally supporting workers who are struggling with current or past substance use issues or returning to the workplace after completing treatment.

While employers care about diversity in their hiring process, knowing where to start and how to integrate hiring those with criminal convictions into your organization is often challenging. Through a tested method of evaluating your company's current practices, Ty can help you navigate whether second chance hiring is right for you and the lowest-risk ways of implementation.

Retaining valued workers with on-the-job troubles related to substance use in the right way is crucial. Engaging Ty's consulting services will assist your company in finding the right balance between compassion and continuing to run an effective business. Ty will provide you with insights into how to help these employees stay on the job, and he will offer techniques to welcome them back into the company after medical leave or treatment to address their issues. With Ty's aid, you can craft an effective and caring way to retain and support your employees.

Recruitment and retention efforts don't have to feel confusing or daunting. To learn more about how Ty Reed can help you, visit his website.

Then text him your name, time zone, and the most convenient time for a free 30- to 60-minute consultation over the phone or Zoom.

https://www.RecoveryAndWork.org/Consulting

(253) 347-1611

# Book Ty Reed to Speak at Your Next Event

When it comes to choosing a professional speaker for your next event, you will find no one more respected or successful—no one who will leave your audience or colleagues feeling more inspired and informed—than Ty Reed, an incredibly gifted professional keynote speaker. Since 2020, Ty has presented to thousands of people across the United States.

Whether your audience is 10 or 10,000, Ty Reed can deliver a customized message of inspiration for your meeting or conference. Ty understands your audience does not want to be "taught" anything, but is rather interested in hearing stories of inspiration, achievement, and real-life people overcoming their struggles.

As a result, Ty Reed's speaking philosophy is to entertain and inspire your audience with passion and stories proven to help people achieve extraordinary results. If you are looking for a memorable speaker who will leave your audience wanting more, book Ty Reed today!

To see videos of Ty Reed and find out whether he is available for your next meeting, visit his site at the address below. Then contact him by phone or email to schedule a complimentary pre-speech phone interview:

www.RecoveryAndWork.org/Speaking
BookTy@RecoveryAndWork.org
(253) 347-1611

www.ingramcontent.com/pod-product-compliance
Lightning Source LLC
Chambersburg PA
CBHW071607200326
41519CB00021BB/6901